Daniela De Luca

ANIMAL ATLAS

MᶜRAE BOOKS

The Animal Atlas was conceived, edited, and designed by McRae Books Srl, Florence, Italy
info@mcraebooks.com

Publishers: Anne McRae, Marco Nardi
Text: Anne McRae
Illustrations: Daniela De Luca
Picture Research: Daniela De Luca
Design: Marco Nardi
Layout and cutouts: Adriano Nardi,
Filippo Delle Monache, Alman (Florence)
Editing: Vicky Egan
Color separations: Litocolor snc (Florence, Italy)

ISBN 88-88166-38-6

Printed and bound in Italy by Artegrafica

Contents

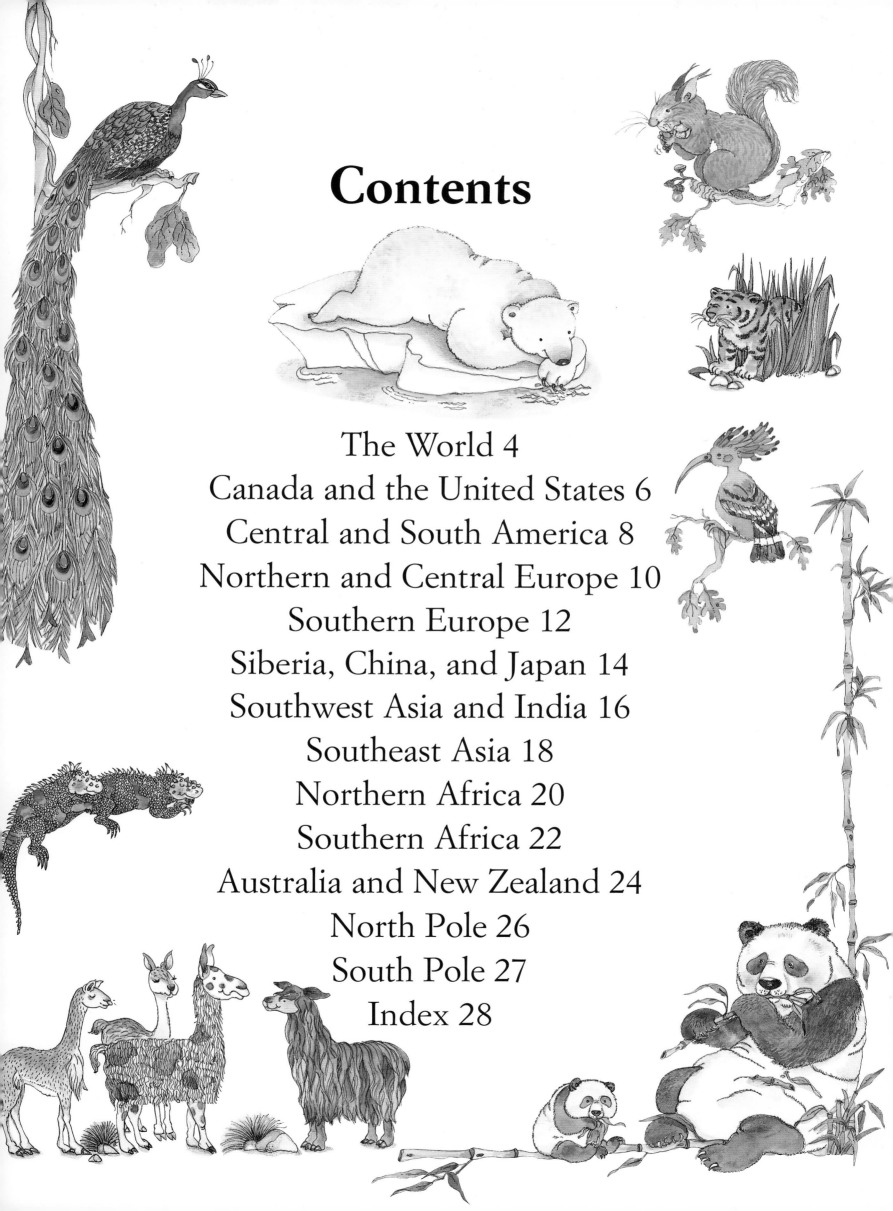

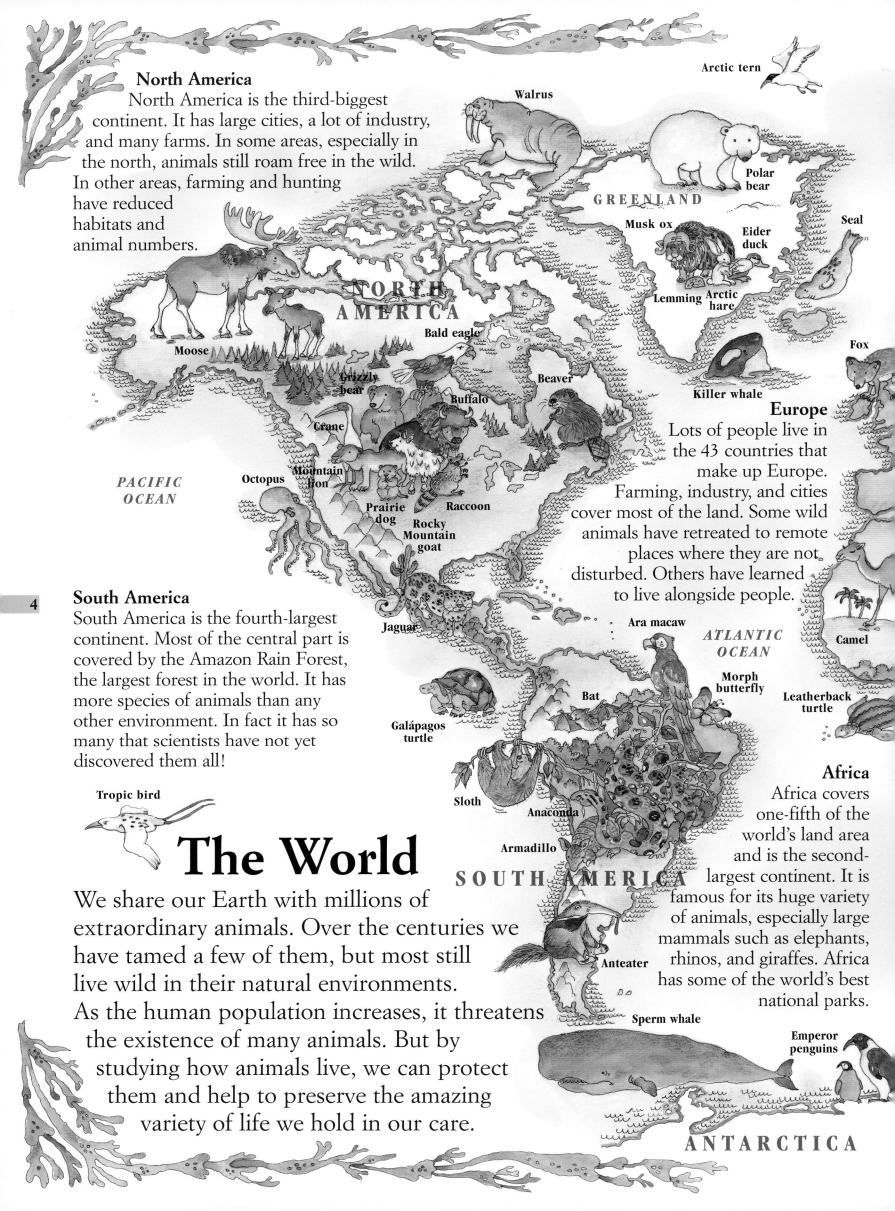

North America

North America is the third-biggest continent. It has large cities, a lot of industry, and many farms. In some areas, especially in the north, animals still roam free in the wild. In other areas, farming and hunting have reduced habitats and animal numbers.

Arctic tern

Walrus

Polar bear

GREENLAND

Musk ox

Eider duck

Seal

Lemming

Arctic hare

NORTH AMERICA

Moose

Bald eagle

Grizzly bear

Buffalo

Beaver

Crane

Killer whale

Fox

PACIFIC OCEAN

Octopus

Mountain lion

Prairie dog

Raccoon

Rocky Mountain goat

Europe

Lots of people live in the 43 countries that make up Europe. Farming, industry, and cities cover most of the land. Some wild animals have retreated to remote places where they are not disturbed. Others have learned to live alongside people.

South America

South America is the fourth-largest continent. Most of the central part is covered by the Amazon Rain Forest, the largest forest in the world. It has more species of animals than any other environment. In fact it has so many that scientists have not yet discovered them all!

Jaguar

Ara macaw

ATLANTIC OCEAN

Camel

Morph butterfly

Leatherback turtle

Bat

Galápagos turtle

Sloth

Anaconda

Armadillo

SOUTH AMERICA

Africa

Africa covers one-fifth of the world's land area and is the second-largest continent. It is famous for its huge variety of animals, especially large mammals such as elephants, rhinos, and giraffes. Africa has some of the world's best national parks.

Tropic bird

The World

We share our Earth with millions of extraordinary animals. Over the centuries we have tamed a few of them, but most still live wild in their natural environments. As the human population increases, it threatens the existence of many animals. But by studying how animals live, we can protect them and help to preserve the amazing variety of life we hold in our care.

Anteater

Sperm whale

Emperor penguins

ANTARCTICA

4

ARCTIC OCEAN

Asia
Asia covers nearly one-third of the Earth's land area, and is the biggest continent. It is separated from Europe by the Ural Mountains. Its animals live in a range of environments, from treeless, frozen tundra to deserts and jungles.

Whale

Owl

Wolf

Reindeer

Deer

EUROPE

URAL MOUNTAINS

ASIA

Brown bear

Peacock

Two-humped camel

Golden monkey

Badger

Wild boar

JAPAN

Tiger

Cobra

Giant panda

Tree shrew

Oceania
Oceania is the name given to the islands scattered across the vast Pacific Ocean, from Australia and New Zealand in the south, to Hawaii in the north. Many unusual animals live on the islands, and the ocean itself teems with life.

AFRICA

Gorilla

Giraffe

5

Rhinoceros

African elephant

PACIFIC OCEAN

Hippopotamus

INDIAN OCEAN

Tapir

Lemur

Kangaroo

AUSTRALIA

Lion

Koala

Frilled lizard

Humpback whale

Platypus

NEW ZEALAND

Albatross

Seas and oceans
Salty water covers nearly three-quarters of the Earth's surface. It is divided into five oceans (the Pacific, the Atlantic, the Indian, the Southern, and the Arctic) and numerous seas. Many animals live in the oceans, from the tiniest algae to giant whales.

White shark

Elephant seal

SOUTHERN OCEAN

Location and land

Northern Canada and Alaska lie within the frozen Arctic Circle. In the west of the region, the Rocky Mountains – one of the world's longest mountain chains – rises in Alaska and runs south to Central America. To the east of the Rockies lie the Great Plains, once the home of huge herds of grazing buffalo. Along the east coast there are forests, and in the southeast are the Florida Everglades – wetland swamps rich in wildlife. Dry deserts cover much of the southwest.

Canada and the United States

Despite its great size, only 10 percent of the world's population lives in North America, which still has many wilderness areas. It has almost every type of environment, from treeless tundra to mountains, forests, grasslands, lakes, rivers, and deserts. But the spread of farming has reduced the wild areas, and fewer animals, such as moose, wolves, and bears, now live there.

The Rocky Mountains

The Rocky Mountains, or Rockies, run the length of the region's west coast. Many of North America's great rivers, such as the Missouri, Rio Grande, and Colorado, start in the Rockies. In the fall, fierce grizzly bears fish in the rivers for salmon. The Rockies are also home to mountain lions, goats, and bighorn sheep.

Prairies and deserts

Central North America is covered in grasslands, or prairies. Once home to vast herds of buffalo and antelope, today they are mainly used as pasture for cattle and sheep. In the southwest of the United States, there are arid deserts dotted with low bushes and cactuses. Reptiles, such as snakes and lizards, are the most common animals in the deserts.

Canada

United States

PACIFIC OCEAN

Central America

ATLANTIC OCEAN

South America

Bighorn sheep

ALASKA (USA)

Moose

CANADA

Porcupine

Rocky Mountain goat

PACIFIC OCEAN

Star-nosed mole

Californian hare

Saguaro cactus

Sea otter

Elf owl

CALIFORNIA

Roadrunner

Blue jay

Grizzly bears

6

ARCTIC OCEAN

GREENLAND

Polar bear

Hooded seal

Opossum

Seal

Crane

Tundra and taiga
In the far north, on the flat tundra, it is too cold for trees to grow. The brief summer lasts only 45 to 60 days, and winters are long and dark. But polar bears, moose, caribou, and seals are able to survive. South of the tundra is a broad band of conifer forest called taiga, where deer, beavers, hawks, and eagles abound.

Sea eagle

Maple

Buffalo

Mountain lion

Beaver

Woodlands
South of the taiga, there are mixed woodlands – home to squirrels, bears, raccoons, and many kinds of birds. Many areas of woodland have been cut down and turned into farmland or cities.

Prairie dog

ATLANTIC OCEAN

UNITED STATES

The Everglades
Subtropical Florida, in the southeast of the region, has a large wetland area of swamps, mangroves, and forests known as the Everglades. The wetlands are home to many wading birds, including herons, egrets, and spoonbills. The American alligator also lives in the swamps. Although the wetlands are protected, many of the animals are endangered.

Tree toad

Raccoon

Mississippi River

Spoonbill

Sage grouse

Rattlesnake

American alligator

Manatee

FLORIDA

Location
The narrow land bridge of Central America is bordered to the north by Mexico (often regarded as part of North America). To the south, Central America hooks on to the vast continent of South America. The tropical Caribbean islands lie to the east, while 600 miles (1,000 kilometers) west of South America are the Galápagos Islands, on the equator.

Tropical rain forest
The Amazon Rain Forest covers some 2.3 million square miles (6 million square kilometers) and is the largest rain forest in the world. More animals and plants live there than in any other place on Earth. The rain forest is a noisy place, especially at dawn, when it is filled with the cries of brightly colored birds and shrieking monkeys.

Grasslands
Vast areas of South America are covered in grassland, which stretches as far as the eye can see. The hot grasslands of the northern lowlands are called llanos. Farther south and east is the pampas. Tapirs, capybaras, rheas, and armadillos are some of the unique grassland animals.

Birds
South America is sometimes called the continent of birds, because so many different species live there. The Andean condor is one of the largest flying birds alive. It soars above the mountains on its huge wings.

ATLANTIC OCEAN

PACIFIC OCEAN

Amazon River

Ara macaw

Emerald tree boa

Silky anteater

Scarlet ibis

Palms

Toucan

Bird-eating spider

Capybara

Golden lion tamarin

Solenodon

Quetzal

Spectacled bear

Bat

Gila monster

Andean condor

North America
Mexico
Central America
Galápagos Islands
Caribbean Islands
South America
ATLANTIC OCEAN
PACIFIC OCEAN

Central and South America

Central and South America are home to about a quarter of all the known species of animals. Most of them live in the huge tropical rain forests that cover almost half the land. There are many rare and unique animals in the region, such as llamas, alpacas, sloths, giant anteaters, jaguars, and capybaras.

Tapirs

Sloth

Poison-arrow frog

Rhea

Armadillo

Jaguar

Silky armadillo

ANDES MOUNTAINS

Chinchilla

Flamingo

Duck

Anteater

The Galápagos Islands

Dotted with volcanoes, the Galápagos Islands are famous for the unusual animals that live there. Many species, like the swimming marine iguanas, are unique – they do not occur anywhere else. Scientists have been able to study how animals on the Galápagos Islands have evolved, or changed, over time.

Darwin's finch

Cactus

Marine iguanas

GALÁPAGOS ISLANDS

Galápagos turtle

Galápagos penguin

Mountain dwellers

The Andes Mountains, the longest mountain chain in the world, sweep down the entire length of western South America. Their slopes and high grassland plateaus are home to llamas, alpacas, guanacos, and vicunas – relatives of the camel, valued for their wool.

Vicuna

Guanaco

Llama

Alpaca

Puffin

ICELAND

Location

This region – northern and central Europe –
extends from Iceland, Ireland, and Britain in
the west, across the great European Plain to
the Ural Mountains in Russia. To the south it
borders Spain, Italy, and the Balkans.

Northern and Central Europe

Northern and Central Europe is a small region with lots of people.
Most of it has a mild, wet climate, but in the far north winters are long
and bitterly cold. Wildlife was once plentiful, and included large
mammals such as hairy mammoths (now extinct), elephants, and
lions. We know this from prehistoric cave paintings that have
been found. Now only a small number
of large mammals survive, including European
bison, elk, and reindeer. Many small
mammals have learned to live
near humans – you can
often see foxes in
city suburbs.

Stoat

Sea gull

Wolverine

Barn owl

NORTH SEA

Stalk

BRITAIN

Fox

Dormouse

IRELAND

BALTIC SEA

Crow

Chamois

10

Forests and woods
Most of Europe was once covered
in thick forests. Many of our
favorite fairy tales, such as *Hansel
and Gretel* and *Little Red Riding
Hood*, take place in these forests.
They were once filled with large
mammals and their predators,
such as elk, reindeer, bears, and
wolves. Smaller animals, including
badgers, squirrels, foxes, hares,
weasels, owls, and blackbirds
were also plentiful. You can still
see all these animals, but their
numbers – and the area of forest
itself – have greatly diminished.

The Alps
The Alps separate northern
Europe from the Mediterranean
countries of southern Europe.
Among their peaks is Mont
Blanc, the tallest mountain in
Europe. Many large rivers start
in the Alps, including the Rhône
and the Rhine. Golden eagles fly
among the peaks, and mountain
hares, ibex, and chamois
graze the slopes.

THE ALPS

Marten

Tundra and conifer forests

The most northern parts of Europe are covered in cold tundra, where only moss, lichen, and low shrubs can grow. Hardy animals such as reindeer and Arctic hares live there. In winter, many tundra animals move south to the conifer forests, where the trees shield them from freezing winds and snow.

Arctic hare

Lemming

Fir tree

Reindeer

Swan

URAL MOUNTAINS

Weasel

Long-eared bat

Brown bear

Owl

Mole

Otter

Volga River

European bison

Green toad

Shrew

CASPIAN SEA

Badger

BLACK SEA

Sturgeon

Rivers

Europe's many large rivers are home to trout and other fish, as well as water birds, otters, beavers, and toads. The Volga River, the longest in Europe, drains into the Caspian Sea. Sturgeon fish that live in the river – some are up to 300 years old – produce roe (eggs), which is sold all over the world as caviar.

Location
Nearly all the countries in southern Europe have a Mediterranean coastline. The largest are Spain, Portugal, France, Italy, Greece, and the Balkan countries (between the Adriatic, Aegean, and Black seas).

ATLANTIC OCEAN

Southern Europe

Asia

Africa

INDIAN OCEAN

Hoopoe

Field mouse

Oak tree

Fallow deer

ATLANTIC OCEAN

Hare

Polecat

F R A N C E

Eagle

Hedgehog

Pyrenean desman

S P A I N

PYRENEES MOUNTAINS

Olive tree

Mouflon

Lynx

P O R T U G A L

Barbary ape

Monk seal

MEDITERRANEAN SEA

Southern Europe

Southern Europe is a dry and sunny region. It was once covered in forests and scrub, and was rich in wildlife. Today, most of the forests have been cleared and the land turned into farmland. Wild animals now live in the mountains and in the remaining patches of scrub and forest. Snakes, lizards, and other reptiles thrive in the region, and hedgehogs, rabbits, mice, and squirrels are among the most common mammals.

Wild boars

Mountain homes

The tallest mountain ranges are the Pyrenees, between Spain and France, and the Alps, which separate Italy from northern Europe. Wild goats and sheep, such as ibex and mouflon, live in the mountains and hills. Wild boars and wild cats, like the lynx, live in the woodlands on the mountain slopes.

Tawny owls

Ibex

Marmot

Red squirrel

Preserving wildlife

National parks and refuges provide safe areas for many endangered species. The Alpine ibex was saved from extinction by the Gran Paradiso National Park in Italy. From there, it was reintroduced to other parts of the Alps. The Doñana National Park in southern Spain has become a refuge for birds. Nearly half the bird species of Europe visit or live in the park.

Deer

Heron

THE ALPS

Night heron

Spoonbill

Hazel mouse

Pine tree

Porcupine

Egyptian vulture

Prickly pear cactus

I T A L Y

T H E B A L K A N S

Green lizard

G R E E C E

Birds

Many birds live in southern Europe, while others pass through as they migrate from the north to Africa and back again. Huge flocks of storks, buzzards, eagles, flamingoes, and many other species can be seen flying overhead at certain times of the year.

The Mediterranean Sea

The warm waters of the Mediterranean Sea teem with fish, birds, and other wildlife. The sea is home to some special animals, such as the monk seal – the rarest seal in the world. Easily disturbed by humans, it survives in tiny, scattered groups.

Sea turtle

Robins

Genet

13

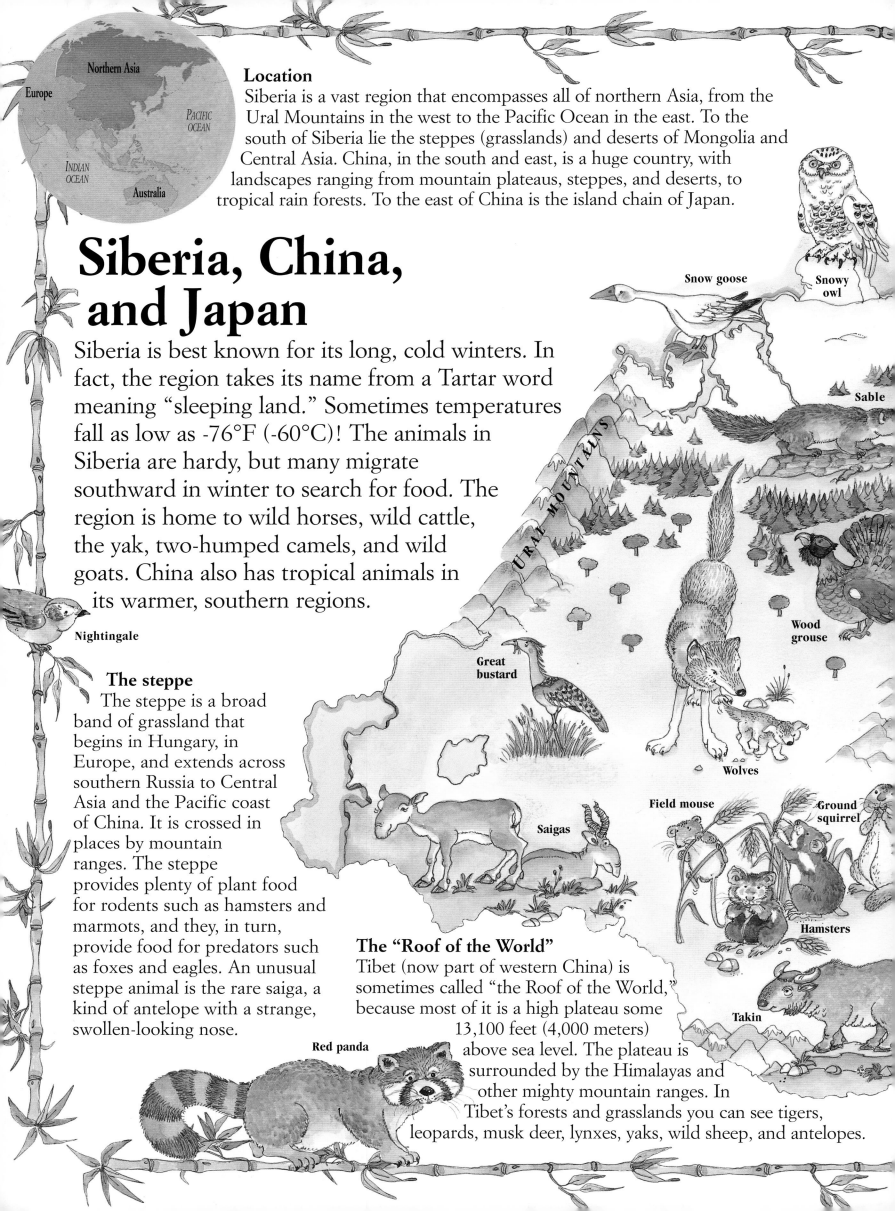

Location

Siberia is a vast region that encompasses all of northern Asia, from the Ural Mountains in the west to the Pacific Ocean in the east. To the south of Siberia lie the steppes (grasslands) and deserts of Mongolia and Central Asia. China, in the south and east, is a huge country, with landscapes ranging from mountain plateaus, steppes, and deserts, to tropical rain forests. To the east of China is the island chain of Japan.

Siberia, China, and Japan

Siberia is best known for its long, cold winters. In fact, the region takes its name from a Tartar word meaning "sleeping land." Sometimes temperatures fall as low as -76°F (-60°C)! The animals in Siberia are hardy, but many migrate southward in winter to search for food. The region is home to wild horses, wild cattle, the yak, two-humped camels, and wild goats. China also has tropical animals in its warmer, southern regions.

Nightingale

The steppe

The steppe is a broad band of grassland that begins in Hungary, in Europe, and extends across southern Russia to Central Asia and the Pacific coast of China. It is crossed in places by mountain ranges. The steppe provides plenty of plant food for rodents such as hamsters and marmots, and they, in turn, provide food for predators such as foxes and eagles. An unusual steppe animal is the rare saiga, a kind of antelope with a strange, swollen-looking nose.

Red panda

The "Roof of the World"

Tibet (now part of western China) is sometimes called "the Roof of the World," because most of it is a high plateau some 13,100 feet (4,000 meters) above sea level. The plateau is surrounded by the Himalayas and other mighty mountain ranges. In Tibet's forests and grasslands you can see tigers, leopards, musk deer, lynxes, yaks, wild sheep, and antelopes.

Northern Asia
Europe
PACIFIC OCEAN
INDIAN OCEAN
Australia

Snow goose
Snowy owl
Sable
URAL MOUNTAINS
Wood grouse
Great bustard
Wolves
Field mouse
Ground squirrel
Saigas
Hamsters
Takin

Beluga and calf

ARCTIC OCEAN

SIBERIA (RUSSIA)

Reindeer

Siberian tiger

Manchurian crane

Baikal seal

Raccoon dog

Two-humped camel

Bamboo

Przewalski's horse

CHINA

Musk deer

Mandarin duck

Alligator

Golden pheasant

JAPAN

Japanese macaque

PACIFIC OCEAN

Giant pandas

Deserts

The Takla Makan and the Gobi are two of the largest deserts in Asia. They are extremely dry, and temperatures range from 113°F (45°C) in summer to -40°F (-40°C) in winter. Few animals live in the Takla Makan, but parts of the Gobi are home to wild camels, horses, asses, gazelles, and antelopes.

Japan

Japan is an island country lying off the east coast of China. Although it is very densely populated, a variety of animals survive in a few remote, mountain forests. There are bears, foxes, deer, wild boars, antelopes, hares, and Japanese macaques.

15

Giant pandas

Giant pandas live in bamboo forests in the mountains of central and western China. For most of the year the forests are shrouded in cloud and mist, and are drenched with heavy rain. The pandas feed on the bamboo. They live alone and have few natural enemies, but they are threatened with extinction because people are clearing the bamboo forests to make farmland.

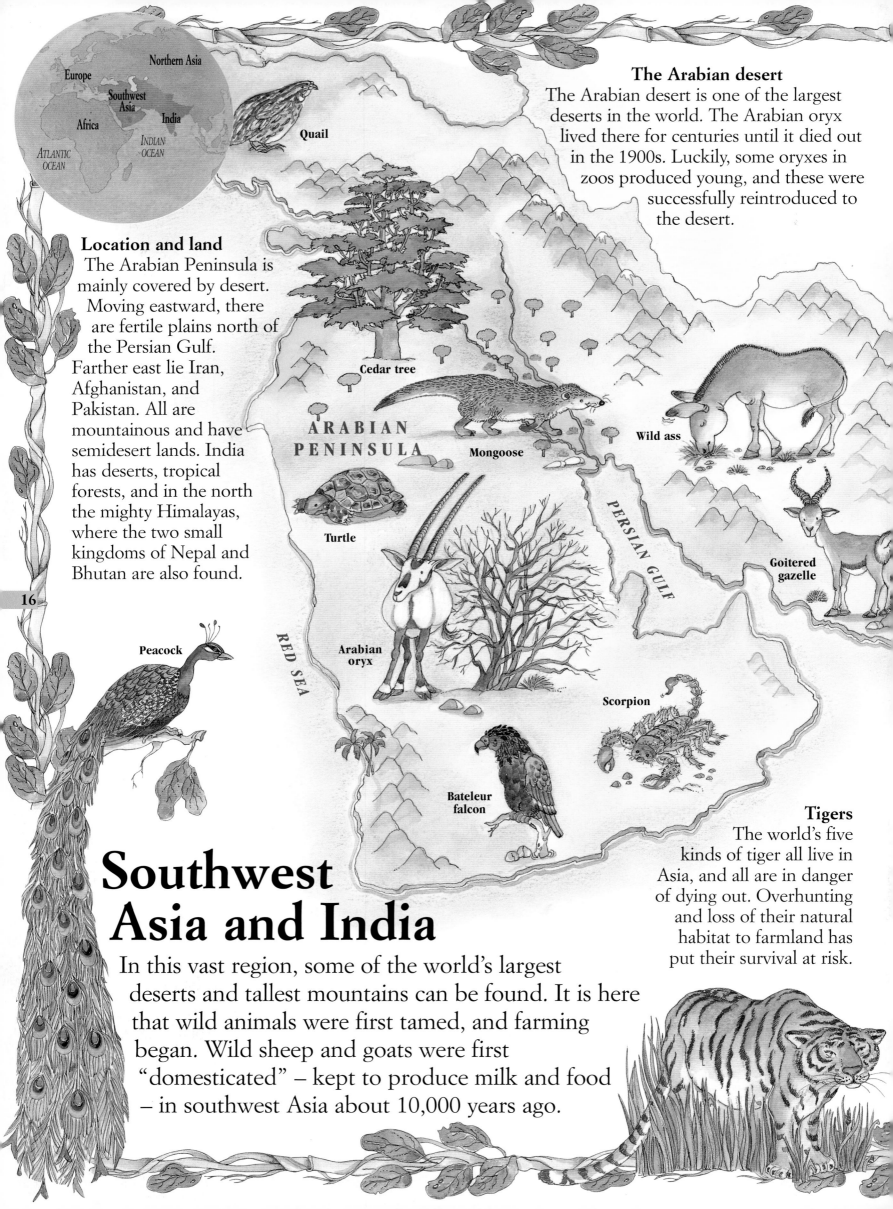

The Arabian desert
The Arabian desert is one of the largest deserts in the world. The Arabian oryx lived there for centuries until it died out in the 1900s. Luckily, some oryxes in zoos produced young, and these were successfully reintroduced to the desert.

Quail

Location and land
The Arabian Peninsula is mainly covered by desert. Moving eastward, there are fertile plains north of the Persian Gulf. Farther east lie Iran, Afghanistan, and Pakistan. All are mountainous and have semidesert lands. India has deserts, tropical forests, and in the north the mighty Himalayas, where the two small kingdoms of Nepal and Bhutan are also found.

Cedar tree

ARABIAN PENINSULA

Mongoose

Wild ass

Turtle

Goitered gazelle

16

Peacock

Arabian oryx

PERSIAN GULF

RED SEA

Scorpion

Bateleur falcon

Tigers
The world's five kinds of tiger all live in Asia, and all are in danger of dying out. Overhunting and loss of their natural habitat to farmland has put their survival at risk.

Southwest Asia and India

In this vast region, some of the world's largest deserts and tallest mountains can be found. It is here that wild animals were first tamed, and farming began. Wild sheep and goats were first "domesticated" – kept to produce milk and food – in southwest Asia about 10,000 years ago.

Northern Asia
Europe
Southwest Asia
Africa
India
ATLANTIC OCEAN
INDIAN OCEAN

Birds of prey

Vultures and eagles are the most common birds of prey in the region. Eagles use their keen eyesight to swoop down on small mammals and reptiles, while vultures feed on carrion – prey that is already dead.

Bearded vulture

Markhor

Snow leopard

Yak

Himalayan black bear

Bhutan glory butterfly

Bobac

Monal pheasant

The Himalayas

The great peaks of the Himalayas include the tallest mountain in the world, Mount Everest, plus 109 others over 24,000 feet (7,300 meters) tall. In the forests on the lower slopes live Himalayan black bears, musk deer, clouded leopards, and Himalayan tahrs. Above the tree line, you can sometimes see snow leopards, yaks, and red pandas. Even higher there are insects and spiders.

Leopard gecko

Pallas's cat

Indus River

Cobra

Himalayan tahr

Langurs

THE HIMALAYAS

Ganges river dolphin

Ganges River

Gavial

Indian rhinoceroses

Fishing owl

Banyan trees

Indian elephants

INDIAN OCEAN

ARABIAN SEA

I N D I A

Palm squirrel

Indian animals

India has a stunning variety of wildlife, including elephants, which live throughout the country. Less easily seen are the three large cat species – the tiger, the cheetah, and the panther. There are also three types of bear and two species of wild pig. Ganges and Indus river dolphins swim in the two great rivers of the same names. Very rare animals include the Asian lion and the Indian rhino.

Tigers

Sloth bear

Wood stork

17

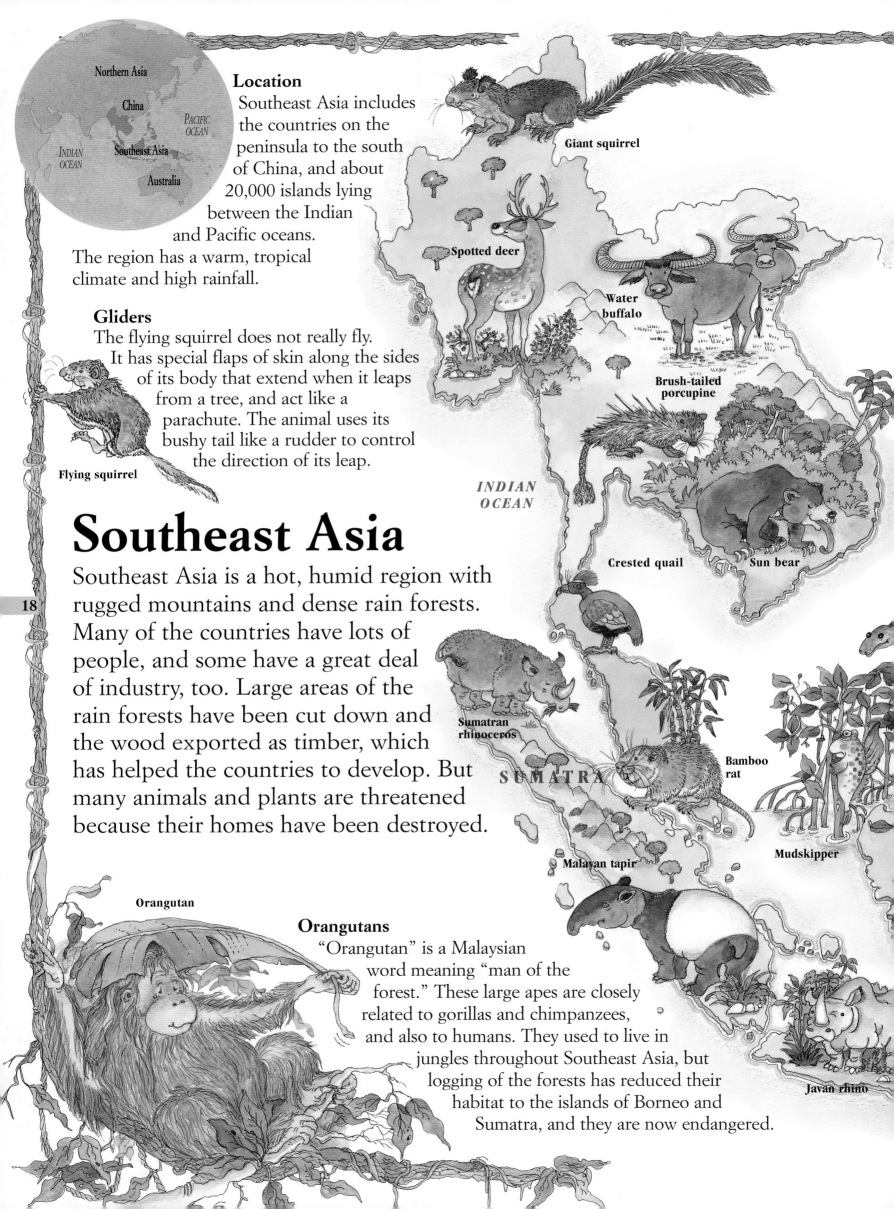

Location

Southeast Asia includes the countries on the peninsula to the south of China, and about 20,000 islands lying between the Indian and Pacific oceans. The region has a warm, tropical climate and high rainfall.

Gliders

The flying squirrel does not really fly. It has special flaps of skin along the sides of its body that extend when it leaps from a tree, and act like a parachute. The animal uses its bushy tail like a rudder to control the direction of its leap.

Flying squirrel

Southeast Asia

Southeast Asia is a hot, humid region with rugged mountains and dense rain forests. Many of the countries have lots of people, and some have a great deal of industry, too. Large areas of the rain forests have been cut down and the wood exported as timber, which has helped the countries to develop. But many animals and plants are threatened because their homes have been destroyed.

Giant squirrel

Spotted deer

Water buffalo

Brush-tailed porcupine

INDIAN OCEAN

Crested quail

Sun bear

Sumatran rhinoceros

SUMATRA

Bamboo rat

Mudskipper

Malayan tapir

Orangutan

Orangutans

"Orangutan" is a Malaysian word meaning "man of the forest." These large apes are closely related to gorillas and chimpanzees, and also to humans. They used to live in jungles throughout Southeast Asia, but logging of the forests has reduced their habitat to the islands of Borneo and Sumatra, and they are now endangered.

Javan rhino

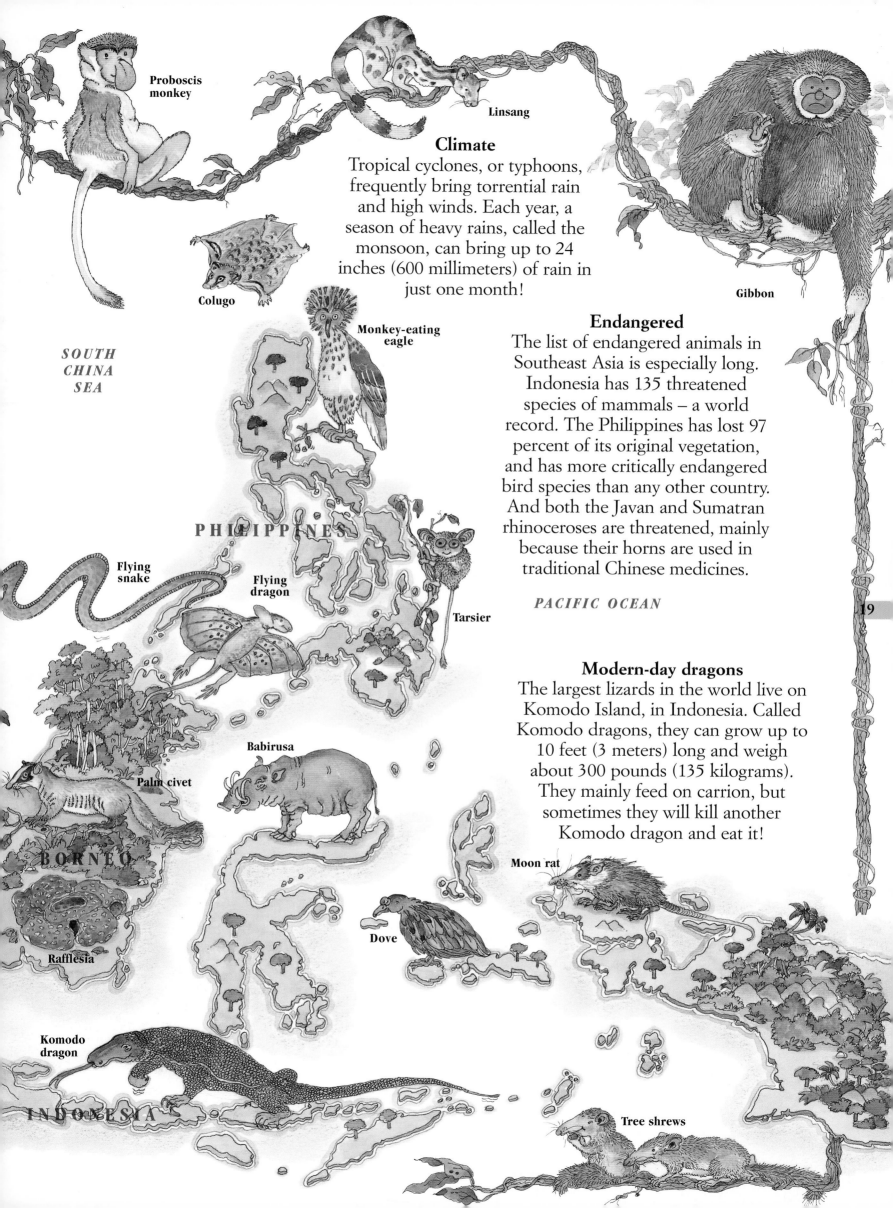

Proboscis monkey

Linsang

Gibbon

Climate
Tropical cyclones, or typhoons, frequently bring torrential rain and high winds. Each year, a season of heavy rains, called the monsoon, can bring up to 24 inches (600 millimeters) of rain in just one month!

Colugo

Monkey-eating eagle

SOUTH CHINA SEA

Endangered
The list of endangered animals in Southeast Asia is especially long. Indonesia has 135 threatened species of mammals – a world record. The Philippines has lost 97 percent of its original vegetation, and has more critically endangered bird species than any other country. And both the Javan and Sumatran rhinoceroses are threatened, mainly because their horns are used in traditional Chinese medicines.

PACIFIC OCEAN

PHILIPPINES

Flying snake

Flying dragon

Tarsier

Modern-day dragons
The largest lizards in the world live on Komodo Island, in Indonesia. Called Komodo dragons, they can grow up to 10 feet (3 meters) long and weigh about 300 pounds (135 kilograms). They mainly feed on carrion, but sometimes they will kill another Komodo dragon and eat it!

Babirusa

Palm civet

Moon rat

BORNEO

Rafflesia

Dove

Komodo dragon

INDONESIA

Tree shrews

19

Location and land

Northern Africa lies south of the Mediterranean Sea. The mighty Nile River, in the east, starts south of the equator and flows northward into the Mediterranean. Most of the central part of northern Africa is covered by the Sahara Desert. This gives way to grassland and tropical forest in the south.

ATLANTIC OCEAN

Europe

Asia

ATLANTIC OCEAN

Northern Africa

INDIAN OCEAN

Horned sheep

Date palms

Jackals

NORTHERN

AHAGGER

Addax

Horned viper

Desert hedgehog

Grazing antelope

Wood stork

Niger River

Tropical forests

The equator crosses Africa just to the south of the region, and the Guinea Coast in the southwest has a hot and humid tropical climate. Lowland rain forest thrives there, mixed with swamps and mangroves. Buffalo wallow in the shallow, muddy waters, and there are countless birds.

African buffalo

Guinea Coast

Pelican

Camels

Adapted for the desert

Camels have many special adaptations that help them to survive in the desert. In the hump on their backs, they have a store of fat that gives them energy when no food is available. They can also survive for many days without water. When they reach a watering hole, they can drink up to 20 gallons (95 liters) in just a few minutes!

MEDITERRANEAN SEA

Sacred ibis

Locust

AFRICA

Nile River

RED SEA

Nile River animals
The Nile, which is about 4,130 miles (6,600 kilometers) long, is the longest river in the world. Many different types of fish live in the river, along with reptiles such as crocodiles, monitor lizards, soft-shelled turtles, and a wide variety of snakes (including two types of cobra).

Desert gerboa

Gerboa

Nile crocodile

Fennec fox

Pharaoh bird

Nile monitor lizard

Dragon tree

Mastigure

Shoebill

Baboon

INDIAN OCEAN

Termite mound

Aardvark

Northern Africa

More than half of northern Africa is covered by the Sahara, the largest desert in the world. Desert animals have special adaptations that enable them to survive in the extreme conditions. Although the landscape may look empty, the animal life is rich and varied. Insects and reptiles have adapted well, but there are also many kinds of birds and mammals. Most animals hide under the sand during the heat of the day and come out at night to eat.

Southern Africa

Southern Africa is home to some of our best loved animals. Here too, many are threatened because their habitats have been turned into farmland. Some are the victims of a terrible trade in live animals – they are sold to zoos, and to people who want them for pets.

Location and land

Rain forests cover the northwest part of southern Africa. East of the rain forests, there are grasslands. To the southeast, lie two large deserts – the Kalahari and the Namib. The region also includes the island of Madagascar.

Rain forest

The Congo River and its many branches flow through the region's dense tropical rain forests. Our closest living relatives – chimpanzees and gorillas – live in these forests. You can also see monkeys, snakes, elephants, buffalo, antelopes, and all kinds of birds in the forests.

Leopard

Cheetah

Lions

Baobab tree

Mount Kilimanjaro

Euphorbia

Wildebeest

Vulture

Marabou stork

Hyena

Python

Goliath toad

Gorilla

Hippopotamus

Chimpanzees

Hornbill

Europe

Asia

Northern Africa

Southern Africa

ATLANTIC OCEAN

INDIAN OCEAN

Madagascar

Madagascar is the fourth-largest island in the world. It lies in the Indian Ocean, off the southeast coast of Africa. Because it has been separated from the mainland for about 50 million years, it has some unique animals, such as lemurs. Lemurs (whose name means "ghosts") come from the same stock as modern monkeys, but have evolved differently.

Pangolin

Lemur

Tenrec

Travelers' palms

Bushpig

INDIAN OCEAN

Warthog

Giraffe

Zebra

Rhinoceros

Acacia tree

Ostriches

Suricate (Meerkat)

Safari!

Southern Africa has some of the most spectacular animals in the world. Many live in national parks and reserves, where they are protected. One of the largest parks is the Serengeti National Park, in Tanzania, in the northeast. It is in this part of Africa that early humans first evolved, and animals have lived there unchanged for at least a million years. Every year in the Serengeti, more than one million wildebeest and 200,000 zebras follow the rains, which move across the land making new pastures grow.

ATLANTIC OCEAN

Chameleon

Ox-pecker

African elephant

The southern deserts

Parts of the Namib Desert never receive any rain at all, and much of the desert has no soil. In contrast, the Kalahari has a good covering of trees, low scrub, and grasses, and is home to elephants, antelope, giraffes, zebras, suricates, and ostriches.

Location
Australia and New Zealand lie in the southern Pacific Ocean. Australia is the largest island in the world, and also the smallest continent. New Zealand has two large islands – North Island and South Island – and many smaller ones. Papua New Guinea, to the north of Australia, covers half the island of New Guinea and includes many smaller islands.

Long-beaked echidna

Bird-of-paradise

ARAFURA SEA

PACIFIC OCEAN

Asia

INDIAN OCEAN

Papua New Guinea

Australia

New Zealand

Cockatoo

INDIAN OCEAN

Crocodile

The land
Australia has a varied landscape, including vast deserts, tropical forests, and cooler areas in the south. New Zealand has large areas of evergreen forest, and a mountain range called the Southern Alps. It also has glaciers and hot springs.

Grass trees

Emu

Dingo

Marsupial mole

Frilled lizard

Cassowary

Moloch

Blue-tongued lizard

A U S T R A L I A

Baobab tree

Uluru (Ayers Rock)

Eastern quoll

Short-beaked echidna

Honey possum

Kangaroo

Wombat

SOUTHERN OCEAN

Platypus

Koalas

Australian animals
Most Australian mammals are marsupials, whose young are born very early and develop in pouches on their mothers' stomachs. Kangaroos, koalas, wombats, and possums are all marsupials. The dingo, a wild dog, was introduced to Australia thousands of years ago by the native Aboriginal people. Australia has several species of poisonous snakes and spiders. Native birds include emus, cockatoos, and many kinds of parrot.

Sugar glider possum

Tasmanian devil

Lorikeets

PAPUA NEW GUINEA

Egg-laying mammals
Echidnas (also called spiny anteaters) and platypuses are the only mammals in the world that lay eggs. They live in Australia and Papua New Guinea.

Giant bat

Sea horse

Great Barrier Reef
The Great Barrier Reef is a chain of islands and coral reefs that runs for 1,240 miles (2,000 kilometers) along the northeast coast of Australia. It teems with colorful wildlife.

Coral

Hermit crab

Clownfish

Octopus

Sea snail

Eucalyptus tree

Bandicoot

Australia and New Zealand

Australia and New Zealand broke away from the rest of the land on the planet millions of years ago, allowing many unique animals to survive or evolve there. Egg-laying mammals, flightless birds, and many kinds of marsupials are some of the region's unusual animals. Today, many native plants and animals are threatened by species such as rats, rabbits, cattle, and sheep, which were introduced by European settlers.

Tasmanian tiger

PACIFIC OCEAN

Blue-footed booby

The tuatara
One of New Zealand's few native reptiles is the tuatara. It is the only survivor of a family of lizard-like creatures that died out 60 million years ago.

Tuatara

TASMAN SEA

NEW ZEALAND

Kakapo

Kea

Kiwi

Takahe

Yellow-eyed penguin

Flightless birds
New Zealand has many flightless birds. Most are in danger of extinction from predators introduced by settlers.

Location and land

The North Pole lies at the center not of a continent, but of a vast sheet of floating ice. This area, with the surrounding northern parts of Scandinavia, Russia, Alaska, and Canada, is known as the Arctic, and lies within the Arctic Circle.

Puffins

Polar bear

Eider duck

Walruses

Arctic hare

Bearded seal

Arctic fox

Living in the cold

Many animals have special ways of keeping warm in the freezing Arctic temperatures. Whales and seals, for example, have a thick layer of fat, called blubber, under their skins to protect them from the icy waters. Polar bears, too, have a layer of fat beneath their thick, shaggy coats. They also have fur on the soles of their feet, and long, curved claws for gripping the frozen ice.

Moss

Lichen

Musk oxen

Seal

North Pole

The North Pole is at the center of the frozen Arctic Ocean. Nothing grows on the frozen ocean, but a range of animals lives there. Nine-tenths of the surrounding lands are free of ice and snow during the summer, and about 900 species of flowering plants burst into bloom at this time.

Narwhal

Good fathers

Emperor penguins nest in the Antarctic. During the coldest month of the year, the females lay a single egg. The males keep it warm by putting it on their feet and tucking it under a fold of skin. Meanwhile, the females go off to sea for two months to feed!

Antarctic waters

The southern seas are rich in squid, fish, and krill – a good source of food for seals, penguins, and whales.

South Pole

The frozen continent around the South Pole is called Antarctica. It is one of the coldest and windiest places on Earth. With an average temperature of -58°F (-50°C), few plants and animals can survive there, although many live in the surrounding seas.

Location

Antarctica lies almost entirely within the Antarctic Circle. It is about one-and-a-half times the size of the United States, and is covered by an ice sheet over a mile deep. Winds of up to 200 miles per hour (320 kilometers per hour) whip the icy continent.

Petrel

Fulmar

Killer whale

Adelie penguin

Leopard seal

Albatross

Weddell seals

Sea elephant

Emperor penguins

Blue whale

ATLANTIC OCEAN

South Pole

PACIFIC OCEAN

Antarctica

INDIAN OCEAN

Index

28